WINTER

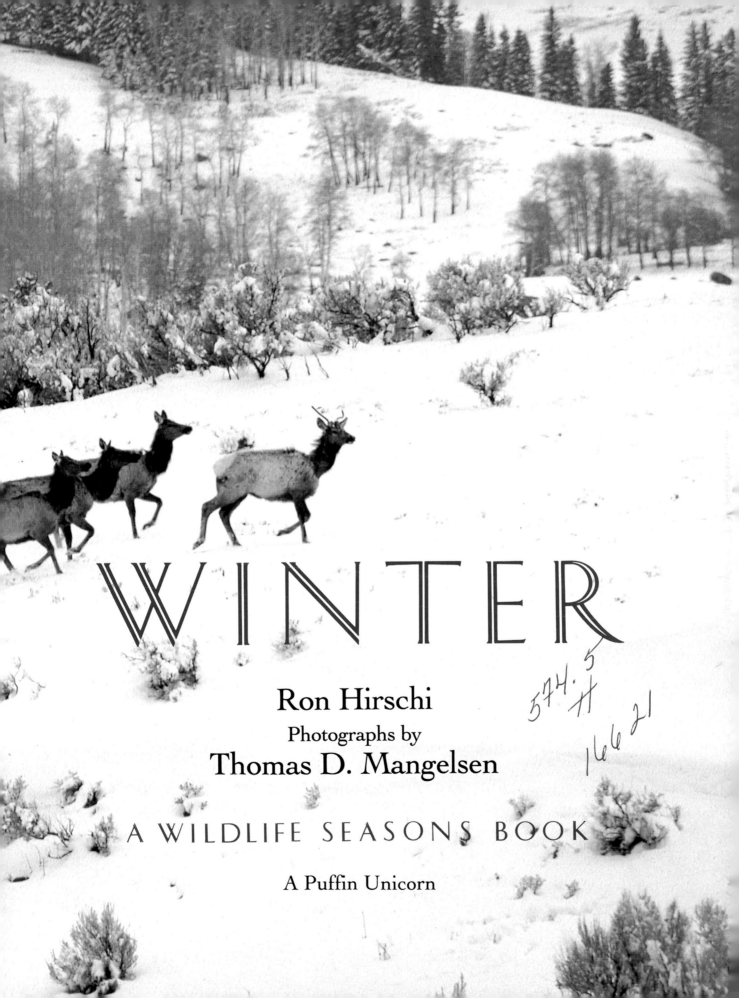

WINTER

Ron Hirschi

Photographs by
Thomas D. Mangelsen

A WILDLIFE SEASONS BOOK

A Puffin Unicorn

PUFFIN UNICORN BOOKS
Published by the Penguin Group
Penguin Books USA Inc., 375 Hudson Street, New York, New York 10014, USA
Penguin Books Ltd, 27 Wrights Lane, London W8 5TZ, England
Penguin Books Australia Ltd, Ringwood, Victoria, Australia
Penguin Books Canada Ltd, 10 Alcorn Avenue, Toronto, Ontario, Canada M4V 3B2
Penguin Books (N.Z.) Ltd, 182-190 Wairau Road, Auckland 10, New Zealand
Penguin Books Ltd, Registered Offices: Harmondsworth, Middlesex, England

First published in the United States by Cobblehill Books,
an affiliate of Dutton Children's Books,
a division of Penguin Books USA Inc., 1990
Published by Puffin Books, 1996

Library of Congress Catalog Card Number: 89-23935
ISBN 0-14-055785-7
Designed by Charlotte Staub
Printed in Hong Kong
10 9 8 7 6 5 4 3 2 1

Winter is also available in hardcover
from Cobblehill Books

For Montana kids. You know best that
time when spring begins...   —R.H.

For my brother David and his children,
Marla, David, and Matthew   —T.M.

Winter is a hush of fallen snow,
a blush of rosy cheeks,
and a time for hot chocolate

after the sleds
are put away.

But out beyond
the edge of town,
winter is weasel white,

Long-tailed weasel

a dance of swimming swans,

Trumpeter swans

Dall sheep

and a time for
thick warm coats
on coyotes and
mountain sheep.

Coyote

Snowy owl

Northern pygmy owl

Great horned owl

Winter is
a season of
waiting owls.

Squirrel tracks

They watch
for mouse
tails twitching,
rabbits leaping,

Cottontail rabbit

Dark-eyed
junco

and tiny birds

Mountain
bluebird

fluffing each feather

Cardinal

Cedar waxwing

to keep out the cold.

Winter is
an icy morning
when all is calm.
All is silent
beneath the deep snow,
inside the marmot's burrow,
and inside the bear's
snug den.

Mountain chickadee

Outside,
the icy branches glisten

while chickadees
search for beetles,
spiders, and caterpillars
that hide in
their cocoons.

Black-capped chickadee

This is the season
for ptarmigan
to hide in feathers
of white,

Willow ptarmigan

Canada geese

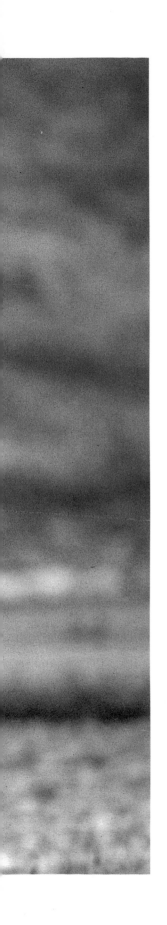

for deer to leap through
the crunching snow,
and for geese to wander
far to the south.

Mule deer

Robin

White-crowned sparrow

Winter is
a time for robins
and sparrows to
search for the last
summer berries,

for moose
to browse
the highest
green
branches.

Bull moose in velvet

And it is a season
that suddenly melts away.
Then springtime appears
like a sleepy bear waking
from its long, long
winter nap.

AFTERWORD

Winter is not an easy time for plants and animals. Freezing weather and vanishing food supplies make life difficult. Some animals avoid this time of ice and snow in unusual ways; bears and marmots hibernate while many birds fly to the south.

Some animals are specially adapted to fit into the winter landscape. Weasels and ptarmigan change fur and feathers to a snow white each year, then shed their winter coats as spring approaches. Swans and many other birds have a dense layer of down feathers to insulate them from the cold. It is hard to imagine how, but tiny birds like the chickadee do keep from freezing their feet when snow blankets the ground.

Flight is probably the most wonderful adaptation to the extremes of winter, and each year thousands of birds migrate short and long distances. Many of these birds fly into backyards where we can have a welcome chance to spend time feeding and getting to know the wildlife of winter. A few sunflowers from summer will help the birds through the cold times. Their songs and bright feathers will offer you a little bit of spring, a chance to dream of the day when winter melts away.

DATE DUE			

574.5
H

Hirschi, Ron.

Winter